Bond

CW00701757

Verbal Reasoning

Assessment Papers

7–8 years

J M Bond

Nelson Thornes

Text © J M Bond 2007
Original illustrations © Nelson Thornes Ltd 2007

The right of J M Bond to be identified as author of this work has been asserted by
her in accordance with the Copyright, Designs and Patents Act 1988.

All rights reserved. No part of this publication may be reproduced or transmitted in
any form or by any means, electronic or mechanical, including photocopy, recording
or any information storage and retrieval system, without permission in writing from
the publisher or under licence from the Copyright Licensing Agency Limited, of
Saffron House, 6–10 Kirby Street, London, EC1N 8TS.

Any person who commits any unauthorised act in relation to this publication may be
liable to criminal prosecution and civil claims for damages.

First published in 1973 by:
Thomas Nelson and Sons Ltd

This edition published in 2007 by:
Nelson Thornes Ltd
Delta Place
27 Bath Road
CHELTENHAM
GL53 7TH
United Kingdom

12 / 10 9 8 7 6 5 4 3 2 1

A catalogue record for this book is available from the British Library

ISBN 978 1 4085 1714 7

Page make-up by Tech Set Ltd

Printed and bound in Egypt by Sahara Printing Company

Before you get started

What is Bond?

This book is part of the Bond Assessment Papers series for verbal reasoning, which provides a **thorough and continuous course in verbal reasoning** from ages six to twelve. It builds up verbal reasoning skills from book to book over the course of the series.

What does this book cover?

Verbal reasoning questions can be grouped into four distinct groups: sorting words, selecting words, anagrams, coded sequences and logic. This book practises a wide range of questions appropriate to the age group drawn from all these categories. One of the key features of Bond Assessment Papers is that each one practises **a very wide variety of skills and question types** so that children are always challenged to think – and don't get bored repeating the same question type again and again. We believe that variety is the key to effective learning. It helps children 'think on their feet' and cope with the unexpected.

The age given on the cover is for guidance only. As the papers are designed to be reasonably challenging for the age group, any one child may naturally find him or herself working above or below the stated age. The important thing is that children are always encouraged by their performance. Working at the right level is the key to this.

What does the book contain?

- **22 papers** – each one contains 30 questions.
- **Scoring devices** – there are scoring boxes next to the questions and a Progress Chart at the back. The chart is a visual and motivating way for children to see how they are doing. Encouraging them to colour in the chart as they go along and to try to beat their last score can be highly effective!
- **Next Steps** – advice on what to do after finishing the papers can be found on the inside back cover.
- **Answers** – located in an easily-removed central pull-out section.

How can you use this book?

One of the great strengths of Bond Assessment Papers is their flexibility. They can be used at home, school and by tutors to:

- provide regular verbal reasoning practice in **bite-sized chunks**
- **highlight strengths and weaknesses** in the core skills
- identify **individual needs**
- set **homework**
- set **timed formal practice tests** – allow about 30 minutes.

It is best to start at the beginning and work through the papers in order

What does a score mean and how can it be improved?

If children colour in the Progress Chart at the back, this will give an idea of how they are doing. The Next Steps inside the back cover will help you to decide what to do next to help a child progress. We suggest that it is always valuable to go over any wrong answers with children.

Don't forget the website...!

Visit www.bond11plus.co.uk for lots of advice, information and suggestions on everything to do with Bond, helping children to do their best, and exams.

Paper 1

1–5 Write the following words in the correct groups.

dog   red   cat   pig   green

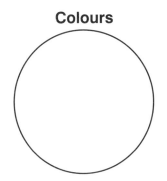

Colours

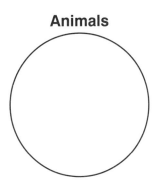

Animals

○ 5

Underline the two words which are made from the same letters.

Example	TAP	PET	<u>TEA</u>	POT	<u>EAT</u>

6 ATE   TAR   TEA   ALE   ARE

7 NAB   BIN   BUN   NOT   NIB

8 TWO   TOO   TOW   WET   TEN

9 NET   TON   NUT   NOT   TAN

10 BAT   BIT   BUT   BET   TUB

○ 5

Change the first word of the third pair in the same way as the other pairs to give a new word.

Example   bind, hind   bare, hare   but, <u>hut</u>

11 pit, pot   lit, lot   hit   _____

12 hit, hat   sit, sat   pit,   _____

13 bat, bet   sat, set   mat,   _____

14 pen, pan   men, man   fen   _____

15 dig, dog   fig, fog   big,   _____

○ 5

(1)

Complete the following sentences by selecting the most sensible word from each group of words given in the brackets. Underline the words selected.

Example The (<u>children</u>, books, foxes) carried the (houses, <u>books</u>, steps) home from the (greengrocer, <u>library</u>, factory).

16 The (house, table, chair) has a (high, tall, big) (garden, doors, curtain).

17 The (dog, baby, kitten) was put in its (bucket, net, pram) ready to be (pushed, chased, rushed) round the park.

18 The (sheep, cow, pig) (barked, crowed, mooed) in the (house, pond, field).

19 The (sky, street, car) was very (delicious, busy, brave).

20 Have you (read, lost, shouted) your (mountain, pen, knee) in the (book, tea, playground)?

5

If the code for TABLE is 1 2 3 4 5, what are the codes for the following words?

21 LET
_____

22 BAT
_____

23 EAT
_____

24 LATE
_____

25 BALE
_____

5

26 Meera is half as old as John. If John is 14, how old is Meera? _____

1

Look at this weather map and answer the questions.

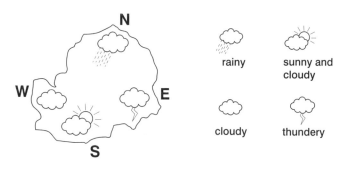

rainy

sunny and cloudy

cloudy

thundery

27 In the north it was _____ .

28 In the south it was _____ .

29 In the west it was _____ .

30 In the east it was _____ .

4

Now go to the Progress Chart to record your score!   Total   30

2

Paper 2

Which one letter can be added to the front of all of these words to make new words?

Example   <u>c</u>are   <u>c</u>at   <u>c</u>rate   <u>c</u>all

1 ___aste   ___ind   ___et   ___ish

2 ___own   ___ust   ___rag   ___ear

3 ___ace   ___ull   ___ind   ___ence

4 ___ond   ___et   ___ound   ___ie

5 ___ang   ___at   ___link   ___ounce   **5**

Put the words below into alphabetical order.

6 DOG   CAT   COW   BULL

_____   _____   _____   _____

Write the words above backwards in alphabetical order.

7 _____   _____   _____   _____   **2**

If the code for BREAD is 1 2 3 4 5, what are the codes for the following words?

8 BAR   9 DAD   10 EAR   11 BAD   12 ADD

_____   _____   _____   _____   _____   **5**

Underline the pair of words most similar in meaning.

Example   come, go   <u>roam, wander</u>   fear, fare

13 break, smash   sand, sea   tea, coffee

14 one, two   brief, short   wet, dry

15 young, old   leg, foot   call, shout

16 green, grass   good, bad   ill, sick

17 tell, story   small, tiny   green, blue   **5**

Tom is 6. He is three years older than Claire and twice as old as Jack. Gareth is one year older than Jack. Gareth has a twin sister, Morwen. How old is:

18 Claire _____   **19** Jack _____

20 Gareth _____   **21** Morwen _____

4

Change one word so that the sentence makes sense. Underline the word you are taking out and write your new word on the line.

> **Example**   I waited in line to buy a <u>book</u> to see the film.   *ticket*

22 I slid down the swings in the park.   _____

23 We baked mum's birthday cake in the freezer.   _____

24 The bicycle arrived at the platform on time.   _____

25 Simon put a date on the envelope and posted it.   _____

4

Underline the one word which **cannot be made** from the letters of the word in capital letters.

> **Example**   S T A T I O N E R Y   stone   ration   <u>nation</u>   noisy

26 STEAK	set	oak	ate	tea
27 CHIPS	ship	hip	sip	fish
28 SNIPE	pen	pea	pin	sip
29 HEART	the	rat	rot	tar
30 WATER	ate	tea	two	tar

5

Paper 3

1–4 Underline any words below which have no two letters the same.

AUNT   BABY   NIECE   UNCLE

LION   SHEEP   MOUSE   STOAT

4

Remove one letter from the word in capital letters to leave a new word. The meaning of the new word is given in the clue.

Example   A U N T   an insect   _ant_

5 READ   a colour   _____

6 HOWL   bird   _____

7 CLUB   young lion   _____

8 CAST   an animal   _____

9 THAT   we wear it   _____

5

10 If May 1st is a Thursday what will the date be on Saturday?   _____

11 If Christmas Day is on a Sunday on which day will Boxing Day (the day after Christmas Day) be?   _____

2

Fill in the missing letters. The alphabet has been written out to help you.

A B C D E F G H I J K L M N O P Q R S T U V W X Y Z

Example   AB is to CD as PQ is to _RS_

12 AB is to CD as EF is to   _____

13 B is to D as F is to   _____

14 BA is to DC as FE is to   _____

15 ABC is to DEF as GHI is to   _____

16 A2 is to B3 as C4 is to   _____

5

Underline the word in the brackets closest in meaning to the word in capitals.

Example UNHAPPY (unkind laughter <u>sad</u> friendly)

17 GO   (out leave come run)

18 FAST   (quick slow stop speed)

19 WET   (dry sun damp clean)

20 CROSS   (kind loving angry frown)

21 WASH   (clean face towel water)

5

Rearrange the muddled letters in capitals to make a proper word. The answer will complete the sentence sensibly.

Example   A BEZAR is an animal with stripes.   <u>ZEBRA</u>

22 The school SUB was late this morning.   _____

23 It is very OLCD today.   _____

24 Where is your ENP?   _____

25 I have lost my KOBO.   _____

26 What time is the YRATP?   _____

5

Four children are going to do some painting.

A and M use yellow paint.   D and E use orange paint.

A and E paint dogs.   D and M paint cats.

27 Who paints yellow dogs?   ____

28 Who paints orange cats?   ____

29 Who paints orange dogs?   ____

30 Who paints yellow cats?   ____

4

Now go to the Progress Chart to record your score!   Total   30

6

1–5 The first six letters of the alphabet are A B C D E F.

Underline the words below which only contain these letters.

feed	bacon	dice	bead
face	back	bread	deaf
faces	call	deal	fade

5

Change one word so that the sentence makes sense. Underline the word you are taking out and write your new word on the line.

Example   I waited in line to buy a <u>book</u> to see the film.   *ticket*

6 The doctor told the children to sit down and hand in their homework.   _____

7 The mouse wagged its tail because it was happy to get a treat.   _____

8 The car drove over a nail and got a flat windscreen.   _____

9 I make my pillow each morning before I go to school.   _____

10 During the storm the tree lost one of its biggest leaves.   _____

5

Underline the two words, one from each group, which are closest in meaning.

Example   (race, shop, <u>start</u>)   (finish, <u>begin</u>, end)

11 (friend, grin, angry)   (kind, smile, sneeze)

12 (up, over, all)   (down, above, top)

13 (bright, dull, sunny)   (storm, cloudy, rain)

14 (silly, tired, bad)   (child, weary, good)

15 (listen, laugh, cry)   (noisy, hear, row)

5

16 The first lesson at school is at 9 o'clock. If it lasts 30 minutes when will it finish? Underline the correct answer in the brackets.

(09:00, 09:15, 09:30)

17 The last lesson of the day ends at 3:30. If it lasts for one hour, when did it start? Underline the correct answer in brackets.

(2:00, 2:30, 3:00)

2

Remove one letter from the word in capital letters to leave a new word. The meaning of the new word is given in the clue.

Example   A U N T   an insect   _ant_

18 BREAK   a part of a bird   _____

19 BLACK   the opposite of front   _____

20 MICE   frozen water   _____

21 LEAST   the opposite of first   _____

22 PLANE   part of a window   _____   5

Complete the following sentences by selecting the most sensible word from each group of words given in the brackets. Underline the words selected.

Example   The (children, books, foxes) carried the (houses, books, steps) home from the (greengrocer, library, factory).

23 My (cat, doll, dog) is wearing a (hard, wooden, spotted) (cup, dish, dress).

24 My (brother, sister, dad) keeps her (book, socks, horse) in the (fridge, road, stable).

25 The (shop, house, pond) closes for (breakfast, lunch, tea).

26 Under the (table, bridge, egg) the (sky, river, castle) was (sleeping, smiling, flowing).

27 Did you (hear, clean, eat) the (chocolate, desk, pencil) that was in the (grass, box, cup)?   5

John and Samina like pets. Rita and Mike like football. Mike and John like biking. Samina and Rita like skateboarding.

28 Who likes football and biking?   _____

29 Who likes pets and biking?   _____

30 Who likes skateboarding and football? _____   3

Underline the two words which are the odd ones out in the following groups of words.

Example   black   <u>king</u>   purple   green   <u>house</u>

1   red   blue   egg   green   cup

2   leaf   rose   daisy   flower   poppy

3   number   one   two   many   four

4   hair   friend   sock   shirt   dress

5   glass   jug   table   cup   chair

5

Change the first word into the last word, by changing one letter at a time and making a new, different word in the middle.

Example   TEN   <u>TIN</u>   FIN

6   PIN   _____   WON

7   LIT   _____   HUT

8   BUY   _____   NUT

9   NOW _____   NET

10   ADD _____   DID

5

Underline two words, one from each group, that go together to form a new word. The word in the first group always comes first.

Example   (hand, <u>green</u>, for)   (light, <u>house</u>, sure)

11   (race, game, post)   (goal, track, way)

12   (flag, room, stair)   (case, wash, pipe)

2

Rearrange the muddled letters to make words.

13   LELB   14   KEIB   15   HIARC

_____   _____   _____

16   ESNP   17   OKHO

_____   _____

5

If a = 2, b = 3, c = 5, d = 6, find the value of these words.

18 a + b = ____

19 a + b + c = ____

20 d − c = ____

3

Give the missing number in each sequence.

    Example   2 4 6 8 <u>10</u>

21 15   12   9   6   ___

22 1   3   ___   7   9

23 4   5   6   7   ___

24 8   7   ___   5   4

4

If the code for STEAM is 7 5 6 4 8, what are the codes for the following words?

25 MAT   _____

26 EAT   _____

27 SEA   _____

28 AM   _____

29 TEA   _____

30 MEAT   _____

6

Now go to the Progress Chart to record your score!   Total 30

Paper 6

Underline the pair of words most opposite in meaning.

	Example	cup, mug	coffee, milk	<u>hot, cold</u>
1	paper, pen	light, dark		book, read
2	bowl, plate	clear, clean		full, empty
3	wild, cross	under, over		wish, like
4	wet, dry	clip, band		hole, full
5	wing, tail	hard, lump		long, short

5

Change the first word of the third pair in the same way as the other pairs to give a new word.

	Example	bind, hind	bare, hare	but, <u>hut</u>
6	red, read	led, lead	bed, _____	
7	fan, flan	can, clan	pan, _____	
8	pop, poop	hop, hoop	lop, _____	
9	sad, sand	bad, band	had, _____	
10	pit, tip	loop, pool	evil, _____	

5

The letters SADM are 1 2 3 4 in code. What do these codes stand for?

11 2 1 1   12 1 2 3   13 2 3 3

_____   _____   _____

14 4 2 3   15 3 2 3

_____   _____

5

16–18 Underline the words which have their letters in alphabetical order. The alphabet has been written out to help you.

A B C D E F G H I J K L M N O P Q R S T U V W X Y Z

DRAW	BOOT	LOST	SPOT
SOCK	HOST	DARK	LION

3

Find the letter which will end the first word and start the second word.

Example   peac (<u>h</u>) ome

19 en (__) ay

20 ar (__) ay

21 si (__) uby

22 li (__) et

23 me (__) wo

( ) 5

Give the missing number in the following sequences.

Example   2 4 6 8 <u>10</u>

24 10	9	8	7	__	5
25 50	__	70	80	90	100
26 2	22	3	33	__	44
27 70	__	60	6	50	5

( ) 4

If $a = 2$, $b = 3$, $c = 4$, $d = 6$, find value of:

28 $c + d =$ ___

29 $a + b + c =$ ___

30 $d - b =$ ___

( ) 3

Paper 7

Complete the following sentences by selecting the most sensible word from each group of words given in the brackets. Underline the words selected.

Example The (children, books, foxes) carried the (houses, books, steps) home from the (greengrocer, library, factory).

1 The (dog, cat, horse) was (cross, hungry, sat) and (mewed, shouted, sang) for her food.

2 The (girl, man, women) drove his (car, bus, whisk) to his (home, bed, kitchen).

3 Her (leg, foot, hand) would not (fit, push, wear) the (hat, coat, shoe).

4 He wanted to (paint, sell, run) his (leg, cows, friend) at the (market, zoo, gallery).

5 When are you going to (catch, tidy, win) the (fish, prize, mess) in your (hair, shoe, room)?

5

6–10 Write the following words in the correct groups.

chairs   cat   stool   mouse   pig

We sit on these   **Animals**

5

Fill in the missing letters and numbers. The alphabet has been written out to help you.

A B C D E F G H I J K L M N O P Q R S T U V W X Y Z

11 A10 is to B8 as C6 is to   _____

12 9B is to 8C as 7D is to   _____

13 AD is to BE as CF is to   _____

14 Z1 is to Y2 as X3 is to   _____

15 AZ is to BY as CX is to   _____

5

Change the first word of the third pair in the same way as the other pairs to give a new word.

Example   bind, hind   bare, hare   but, <u>hut</u>

16   rip, dip   ray, day   rot, _____

17   can, cat   ban, bat   fan, _____

18   fad, fed   bad, bed   lad, _____

19   cot, cat   rot, rat   pot, _____

20   nip, nap   lip, lap   tip, _____   5

Find the letter which will end the first word and start the second word.

Example   peac (<u>h</u>) ome

21   wir (____) nd

22   sno (____) ork

23   nes (____) ime

24   ca (____) wo

25   bu (____) es   5

If a = 1, b = 2, c = 3, d = 5, find the value of:

26   a + b + c = ____

27   d − c =   ____

28   b + c + d = ____   3

Sarah gets three times as much pocket money as Raj got two years ago. Raj's pocket money goes up by £1 a year. He now gets £3 a week.

29   How much did Raj get two years ago?   ____

30   How much does Sarah get?   ____   2

Paper 8

Which one letter can be added to the front of all of these words to make new words?

Example $\underline{c}$ are $\underline{c}$ at $\underline{c}$ rate $\underline{c}$ all

1 ___lean   ___ase   ___heap   ___row

2 ___and   ___one   ___end   ___in

3 ___ear   ___hip   ___hen   ___asp

4 ___eat   ___ole   ___ard   ___ouse

5 ___able   ___ray   ___hen   ___an

5

Underline the word in the brackets closest in meaning to the word in capitals.

Example UNHAPPY (unkind   laughter   <u>sad</u>   friendly)

6 RULER   (crown   queen   palace   straight)

7 BOY   (child   toddler   lad   baby)

8 BOAT   (sailor   sea   ocean   ship)

9 JUMP   (cross   run   leap   fall)

10 HARD   (easy   difficult   nasty   solid)

5

In each line, underline the word which would come third if the words were placed in alphabetical order.

11 Sanjay   Mike   Rita   Amin   Claire

12 London   Bath   York   Truro   Paris

13 spoon   pencil   knife   scissors   crayon

14 frog   newt   fish   tadpole   beetle

15 mice   nail   tree   apple   zebra

5

Complete the following expressions by underlining the missing word.

Example Frog is to tadpole as swan is to (duckling, baby, <u>cygnet</u>).

16 Grass is to green as snow is to (blue, white, brown).

17 Fire is to red as sea is to (blue, brown, rough).

18 Cat is to kitten as dog is to (poodle, puppy, dog).

19 Water is to drink as bread is to (eat, plate, cup).

20 July is to June as May is to (June, April, March).

5

Choose the word or phrase that makes each sentence true.

Example A LIBRARY always has (posters, a carpet, <u>books</u>, DVDs, stairs).

21 A TREE always has (flowers, a bird feeder, berries, roots, leaves).

22 A VILLAGE always has (a petrol station, an airport, houses, a leisure centre, a clothing shop).

23 A TELEVISION always has (a stand, a DVD player, a remote control, a screen, a video recorder).

24 A GARDEN CENTRE always has (a restaurant, books, plants, swing sets, customers).

25 A SANDWICH always has (cheese, lettuce, butter, bread, ham).

5

Find a word that is similar in meaning to the word in capital letters and that rhymes with the second word.

Example CABLE   tyre   *wire*

26 RENT   spire   _____

27 FRIEND   late   _____

28 WOOLLY ANIMAL   sleep   _____

29 MIDDAY   spoon   _____

30 PIPS   leads   _____

5

Paper 9

Find a word that can be put in front of each of the following words to make new, compound words.

	Example	CAST	FALL	WARD	POUR	DOWN
1	CAKE	CUP	POT	ROOM	_____	
2	LID	PATCH	BALL	SIGHT	_____	
3	SHIP	LIGHT	FISH	BURST	_____	
4	LONG	LAMP	ACHE	BAND	_____	
5	CHILD	FATHER	STAND	PARENT	_____	

5

Find a word that is similar in meaning to the word in capital letters and that rhymes with the second word.

	Example	CABLE	tyre	wire
6	VEHICLE	far	_____	
7	A ROAD	meet	_____	
8	GROCERIES	mood	_____	
9	SPONGE	make	_____	

4

Sue and Paul have chips. Colin and Anna have pizza.
Anna and Sue put salt on their food. Paul and Colin put ketchup on their food.

10 Who puts salt on their chips? _____

11 Who puts ketchup on their pizza? _____

12 Who puts ketchup on their chips? _____

13 Who puts salt on their pizza? _____

4

Change one word so that the sentence makes sense. Underline the word you are taking out and write your new word on the line.

Example   I waited in line to buy a <u>book</u> to see the film.   *ticket*

14 The pilot asked the passengers to stay in their seats because the train was about to take off.   _____

15 Lemar put the key in the roof and opened the door to his flat.   _____

16 My mum likes a hot cup of tea when she gets up each evening.   _____

17 The girls' netball team cheered when they lost the match.   _____

18 'Please hurry or we're going to be early for school.'   _____   **5**

If the code for MASTER is 9 5 8 6 7 1, what are the codes for the following words?

19 MAT   _____

20 TEA   _____

21 ARM   _____

22 MAR   _____

23 RAT   _____   **5**

Change the first word into the last word, by changing one letter at a time and making a new, different word in the middle.

Example   TEN   <u>TIN</u>   FIN

24 PUN   _____   MAN

25 SON   _____   BUN

26 MET   _____   MAY

27 MIX   _____   FOX

28 POT   _____   PEN   **5**

Kim is in the drama club which meets on Tuesday and Thursday. She is also in the swimming club which meets on Wednesday. On Monday and Thursday, Kim has piano lessons.

29 On which day does Kim have the most activities?   _____

30 On which school day does Kim not have any activities?   _____   **2**

Paper 10

Underline the pair of words most similar in meaning.

Example   come, go   <u>roam, wander</u>   fear, fare

1 warm, sunny   good, luck   dark, light

2 long, walk   high, jump   thin, slim

3 middle, centre   rough, dry   weak, strong

4 alley, lane   real, false   back, front

5 awake, asleep   tidy, neat   bake, oven

5

Find the letter which will end the first word and start the second word.

Example   peac (<u>h</u>) ome

6 ad (—) en

7 to (—) lf

8 sa (—) ou

9 fi (—) ew

10 od (—) ad

5

Remove one letter from the word in capital letters to leave a new word. The meaning of the new word is given in the clue.

Example   A U N T   an insect   <u>ant</u>

11 STING   something a pop star can do   _____

12 HAUNT   a relation   _____

13 FLEET   part of our body   _____

14 HOARD   not soft   _____

15 SHOE   a garden tool   _____

5

Complete the following sentences by selecting the most sensible word from each group of words given in the brackets. Underline the words selected.

Example   The (<u>children</u>, books, foxes) carried the (houses, <u>books</u>, steps) home from the (greengrocer, <u>library</u>, factory).

16 The girl (tore, put on, cut) her (overall, dress, apron) and went to the (bath, kitchen, cook).

17 The (birds, bees, flowers) needed (sweeping, brushing, watering) as they were very (wet, dry, cold).

18 The (rider, player, walker) kicked the (ground, ball, horse) into the (hole, house, goal).

19 The small (horse, mouse, fly) squeezed into its (bed, hole, trap) and ate the (cheese, spring, fish).

20 The (flock, crowd, team) (ate, stole, scored) three (houses, goals, frogs). ⬤ 5

If the code for CREATE is 5 6 4 8 9 4, what do these codes stand for?

21 589   _____

22 489   _____

23 865   _____

24 948   _____

25 6894   _____   ⬤ 5

In a test of 40 questions there was one mark for each correct answer. Write down the number of marks each person got.

26 C got half right.   __

27 B got 3 more than C.   __

28 D got 2 less than C   __

29 E got 2 less than D.   __

30 A had only 1 mistake.   __   ⬤ 5

Now go to the Progress Chart to record your score!   Total ⬤ 30

Complete the following expressions by underlining in the missing word.

Example   Frog is to tadpole as swan is to (duckling, baby, <u>cygnet</u>).

1 People are to house as car is to (hens, garage, paint).

2 Skip is to rope as cricket is to (stick, bat, net).

3 Cats are to mew as dogs are to (bones, lead, bark).

4 Car is to road as train is to (station, rails, engine).

5 Man is to foot as lion is to (foot, paw, paddle).

5

Which one letter can be added to the front of all of these words to make new words?

Example	<u>c</u>are	<u>c</u>at	<u>c</u>rate	<u>c</u>all
6 __late	__an	__op	__lane
7 __lag	__ool	__ig	__lower
8 __ing	__heel	__ipe	__ater
9 __lad	__low	__rip	__un
10 __all	__ank	__ime	__ower

5

Change one word so that the sentence makes sense. Underline the word you are taking out and write your new word on the line.

Example   I waited in line to buy a <u>book</u> to see the film.   *ticket*

11 Turn the lamp on. It's light in here!   _____

12 It was so cold, Mia lit the fan to keep warm.   _____

13 The rain blew the leaves off the trees.   _____

14 The airline pilot sailed over the sea in his plane.   _____

4

Underline the one word which **cannot be made** from the letters of the word in capital letters.

Example   S T A T I O N E R Y   stone   ration   <u>nation</u>   noisy

15 CLOSED   sold   cold   dose   seed

16 CHARGE   gear   have   cage   race

17 FRIEND   fired   fend   deaf   find

18 OLIVES   live   vest   sole   lies

19 INVENTS   nine   nest   even   vine   5

20 My watch is 5 minutes slow and it shows 12:30.

What is the right time?   _____

21 If I had 20p more I would have twice as much as my sister who has 50p.

How much have I now?   _____   2

Fill in the missing numbers and letters in each sequence.

Example   2   4   6   8   <u>10</u>

22 33   30   ___   24   21   18

23 A9   B8   C7   ___   E5   F4

24 6   11   16   ___   26   31

25 3   7   11   15   19   ___   4

Underline the word in the brackets closest in meaning to the word in capitals.

Example   UNHAPPY   (unkind   laughter   <u>sad</u>   friendly)

26 CLEVER   (teacher   school   bright   dull)

27 STORY   (tale   read   book   paper)

28 MEAL   (table   chair   dinner   eat)

29 ALWAYS   (never   sometimes   hour   forever)

30 END   (start   finish   race   entry)   5

Paper 1

1–5 *Colours:* red, green
Animals: dog, cat, pig
6 ATE, TEA
7 BIN, NIB
8 TWO, TOW
9 TON, NOT
10 BUT, TUB
11 hot
12 pat
13 met
14 fan
15 bog
16 house, big, garden
17 baby, pram, pushed
18 cow, mooed, field
19 street, busy
20 lost, pen, playground
21 451
22 321
23 521
24 4215
25 3245
26 7
27 rainy
28 sunny and cloudy
29 cloudy
30 thundery

Paper 2

1 w
2 d
3 f
4 p
5 b
6 BULL, CAT, COW, DOG
7 GOD, LLUB, TAC, WOC
8 142
9 545
10 342
11 145
12 455
13 break, smash
14 brief, short
15 call, shout
16 ill, sick
17 small, tiny
18 3
19 3
20 4
21 4
22 <u>swings</u>, slide
23 <u>freezer</u>, oven
24 <u>bicycle</u>, train
25 <u>date</u>, stamp
26 oak
27 fish
28 pea
29 rot
30 two

Paper 3

1 AUNT
2 UNCLE
3 LION
4 MOUSE
5 red
6 owl
7 cub
8 cat
9 hat
10 May 3rd
11 Monday
12 GH
13 H
14 HG
15 JKL
16 D5
17 leave
18 quick
19 damp
20 angry
21 clean
22 BUS
23 COLD
24 PEN
25 BOOK
26 PARTY
27 A
28 D
29 E
30 M

ANSWERS

ANSWERS

Paper 4

1–5 feed, bead, face, deaf, fade
6 <u>doctor</u>, teacher
7 <u>mouse</u>, dog
8 <u>windscreen</u>, tyre
9 <u>pillow</u>, bed
10 <u>leaves</u>, branches
11 grin, smile
12 over, above
13 dull, cloudy
14 tired, weary
15 listen, hear
16 09:30
17 2:30
18 beak
19 back
20 ice
21 last
22 pane
23 doll, spotted, dress
24 sister, horse, stable
25 shop, lunch
26 bridge, river, flowing
27 eat, chocolate, box
28 Mike
29 John
30 Rita

Paper 5

1 egg, cup
2 leaf, flower
3 number, many
4 hair, friend
5 table, chair
6 WIN
7 HIT
8 BUT
9 NEW or NOT
10 AID
11 racetrack
12 staircase
13 BELL
14 BIKE
15 CHAIR
16 PENS
17 HOOK
18 5
19 10
20 1
21 3
22 5
23 8
24 6
25 845
26 645
27 764
28 48
29 564
30 8645

Paper 6

1 light, dark
2 full, empty
3 under, over
4 wet, dry
5 long, short
6 bead
7 plan
8 loop
9 hand
10 live
11 ASS
12 SAD
13 ADD
14 MAD
15 DAD
16–18 BOOT, LOST, HOST
19 d
20 m
21 r
22 p
23 t
24 6
25 60
26 4
27 7
28 10
29 9
30 3

Paper 7

1. cat, hungry, mewed
2. man, car, home
3. foot, fit, shoe
4. sell, cows, market
5. tidy, mess, room
6–10. *We sit on these:* chairs, stool
   Animals: cat, mouse, pig
11. D4
12. 6E
13. DG
14. W4
15. DW
16. dot
17. fat
18. led
19. pat
20. tap
21. e
22. w
23. t
24. t
25. y
26. 6
27. 2
28. 10
29. £1
30. £3

Paper 8

1. c
2. b
3. w
4. h
5. t
6. queen
7. lad
8. ship
9. leap
10. difficult
11. Mike
12. Paris
13. pencil
14. frog
15. nail
16. white
17. blue
18. puppy
19. eat
20. April
21. roots
22. houses
23. a screen
24. plants
25. bread
26. hire
27. mate
28. sheep
29. noon
30. seeds

Paper 9

1. TEA
2. EYE
3. STAR
4. HEAD
5. GRAND
6. car
7. street
8. food
9. cake
10. Sue
11. Colin
12. Paul
13. Anna
14. train, plane
15. roof, lock
16. evening, morning
17. lost, won
18. early, late
19. 956
20. 675
21. 519
22. 951
23. 156
24. PAN
25. SUN
26. MAT
27. FIX
28. PET
29. Thursday
30. Friday

Paper 10

1 warm, sunny
2 thin, slim
3 middle, centre
4 alley, lane
5 tidy, neat
6 d
7 e
8 y
9 n
10 d
11 sing
12 aunt
13 feet
14 hard
15 hoe
16 put on, apron, kitchen
17 flowers, watering, dry
18 player, ball, goal
19 mouse, hole, cheese
20 team, scored, goals
21 CAT
22 EAT
23 ARC
24 TEA
25 RATE
26 20
27 23
28 18
29 16
30 39

Paper 11

1 garage
2 bat
3 bark
4 rails
5 paw
6 p
7 f
8 w
9 g
10 t
11 light, dark
12 fan, fire
13 rain, wind
14 sailed, flew
15 seed
16 have
17 deaf
18 vest
19 even
20 12:35
21 80p
22 27
23 D6
24 21
25 23
26 bright
27 tale
28 dinner
29 forever
30 finish

Paper 12

1 A
2 J
3 M
4 P
5 girl
6 morning
7 go
8 double
9 cold
10 burgle, steal
11 truck, lorry
12 talk, chat
13 start, begin
14 quick, fast
15 tame
16 heat
17 host
18 cheap
19 black
20 13
21 £1
22 ARM, RAM
23 LOW, OWL
24 WON, NOW
25 CAR, ARC
26 DAB, BAD
27 C6
28 24
29 6
30 ae

1   Geoffrey
2   18th December
3   November
4   WIN
5   HIT
6   BUT
7   RIB
8   HAT
9   wide, broad
10 shut, closed
11 gift, present
12 tall, high
13 peaceful, calm
14 465
15 536
16 624
17 2653
18 5362
19 CAT
20 FISH
21 DOG
22 MEAT
23 BARKS
24 sat, mended, bike
25 cold, blowing, outside
26 played, game, computer
27 swimmer, dived, pool
28 clock, ticked, shelf
29 car
30 pudding

1   Tom
2   Leo
3   5, 2, 1, 3, 4
4   1, 3, 5, 2, 4
5   3, 1, 2, 5, 4
6   3, 2, 1, 4, 5
7   sad, sorry
8   neat, tidy
9   laugh, chuckle
10 glad, happy
11 above, over
12 533
13 253
14 265
15 3654
16 35462
17 trace
18 told
19 trade
20 comet
21 health
22 pasta, water
23 parade, street
24 homework, his
25 shoes, two
26 fun
27 dot
28 set
29 nut
30 ace

1–5 *Vegetables:* leeks, peas
    Colours: yellow, brown, pink
6   DOG
7   LAMB
8   PONY
9   GOAT
10 CAT
11 lock
12 each
13 old
14 ears
15 nets
16 book
17 game
18 school
19 car
20 seagull
21 DEED
22 FACED
23 DEAF
24 FEED
25 2
26 6
27 13
28 train, catch
29 tree, wind
30 final, goal

ANSWERS

Paper 16

1 tint
2 chat
3 west
4 beat
5 ears
6 m
7 t
8 k
9 f
10 h
11 sand
12 link
13 bake
14 hoot
15 pan
16 read, magazine, bed
17 enjoyed, colourful, fireworks
18 left, clothes, bathroom
19 boat, tossed, sea
20 horses, neighed, stable
21 18
22 21
23 2
24 3
25 8
26 seagull
27 fairground
28 flagpole
29 network
30 paintbox

Paper 17

1 mane
2 pen
3 tall
4 wall
5 and
6 story
7 stride
8 shatter
9 journey
10 uproar
11 soft
12 tame
13 lost
14 loud
15 e
16 s
17 w
18 t
19 t
20 c
21 a
22 c
23 9531
24 5981
25 13538
26 SET
27 TAN
28 Robin
29 Megan
30 Mark

Paper 18

1 r
2 p
3 s
4 h
5 d
6 bike, track
7 the, into
8 harness, dog
9 cold, fingers
10 water, sea
11 stool, chair
12 paper, rubber
13 house, cottage
14 sea, ocean
15 12
16 123
17 423
18 325
19 1236
20 t
21 l
22 d
23 l
24 r
25 m
26 l
27 d
28 g
29 h
30 e

Paper 19

1. d
2. l
3. n
4. f
5. w
6. chair, floral, material
7. pictures, walls, room
8. ever, sea, dolphins
9. dragon, scales, back
10. squeezed, gate, quickly
11. jungle, zoo
12. foot, hand
13. blunt, sharp
14. wear
15. rest
16. near
17. wasp
18. hens
19. lamp
20. read
21. frog
22. nest
23. mast
24. shut
25. lamb
26. hand
27. small
28. out
29. 2, 1, 3, 5, 4
30. 5, 3, 2, 1, 4

Paper 20

1. hound
2. fight
3. start
4. mouse
5. crate
6. t
7. t
8. g
9. p
10. d
11. bat
12. pain
13. harp
14. race
15. bear
16. weak
17. ill
18. low
19. hot
20. last
21. Q
22. LEAD
23. DAME
24. D
25. Friday
26. Wednesday
27. SEA
28. LIFE
29. BLACK
30. BATTLE

Paper 21

1.

R	A	T
A	G	O
M	A	P

2.

B	I	N
A	C	E
G	E	T

3. blind
4. coast
5. slow
6. bald
7. learn
8. IDC
9. FHI
10. DFH
11. FHAC
12. IDCHA
13–17 *Vegetables (A)*: leeks, onions
Buildings (B): house, school
Things we do (C): cycle, run, write
Birds (D): owl, lark, swan
(give one mark for each two correct)
18. WHEN
19. FLYING
20. INDIA
21. QUICK
22. CINEMA
23. bag, DVDs, library
24. touch, fence, electric
25. sea, crashing, shore
26. gobbled, pudding, greedily
27. postman, parcel
28. Thursday
29. 12:25
30. 15th

ANSWERS

Paper 22

1 d
2 n
3 t
4 l
5 n
6 jawbone
7 bagpipes
8 drawbridge
9 feast
10 frail
11 plant
12 plate
13 slip
14 speak
15 fright
16 teach
17 scratch
18 stream
19 train
20 coast
21 cat
22 sea
23 car
24 hen
25 water
26 BXQ
27 PXQ
28 LPF
29 GEAR
30 RANG

Paper 12

A and M were tall. J and P were short. M and J were fair and A and P were dark.

   1 Who was tall and dark?   —

   2 Who was short and fair?   —

   3 Who was tall and fair?   —

   4 Who was short and dark?   —

4

Complete the following expressions by underlining the missing word.

   Example   Frog is to tadpole as swan is to (duckling, baby, <u>cygnet</u>).

   5 Man is to woman as boy is to (child, son, girl).

   6 Night is to day as evening is to (lunch, morning, sunset).

   7 Red is to stop as green is to (danger, go, wait).

   8 One is to single as two is to (three, double, mix).

   9 Oven is to hot as refrigerator is to (shelf, food, cold).

5

Underline the two words in each line which are most similar in type or meaning.

   Example   <u>dear</u> pleasant poor extravagant <u>expensive</u>

   10 rough burgle even steal hungry

   11 truck car train lorry bike

   12 talk listen put aunt chat

   13 start close late stop begin

   14 quick slow steady fast walk

5

Change the first word of the third pair in the same way as the other pairs to give a new word.

Example   bind, hind   bare, hare   but, <u>hut</u>

15 some, same   dome, dame   tome, _____

16 four, hour   fang, hang   feat, _____

17 lair, hair   lint, hint   lost, _____

18 clan, clean   dram, dream   chap, _____

19 pace, place   sing, sling   back, _____   **5**

20 In 3 years time Shen will be twice as old as I am now.
If I am 8 now how old is Shen?   ___

21 If I had 20p more I would have twice as much as my sister who has 60p. How much have I?   ___   **2**

Underline the two words which are made from the same letters.

Example   TAP   PET   <u>TEA</u>   POT   <u>EAT</u>

22 ARM   RIM   AIR   RUM   RAM

23 PIT   LOW   PET   OWL   LET

24 WON   OUT   NOW   WIN   HIM

25 BUS   CAR   ARK   FOX   ARC

26 MAN   CUT   DAB   DIM   BAD   **5**

Fill in the missing numbers and letters in each sequence.

Example   2   4   6   8   <u>10</u>

27 A10   B8   ___   D4   E2   F0

28 28   ___   20   16   12   8

29 3   ___   9   12   15   18

30 ab   ac   ad   ___   af   ag   **4**

My brother's name begins with the 7th letter of the alphabet.

1 Is it Francis, Henry or Geoffrey? _____

2 His birthday is exactly a week before Christmas Day.

Is it the 16th, 17th or 18th December? _____

3 My birthday is in the month beginning with the 14th letter of the alphabet.

Is it in October, November or March? _____

3

Change the first word into the last word, by changing one letter at a time and making a new, different word in the middle.

Example   TEN   TIN   FIN

4 PIN _____ WON

5 LIT _____ HUT

6 BUY _____ NUT

7 RUB _____ BIB

8 HAY _____ PAT

5

Underline the two words, one from each group, which are closest in meaning.

Example   (race, shop, <u>start</u>)   (finish, <u>begin</u>, end)

9 (large, slow, wide)   (broad, quick, small)

10 (sound, shut, people)   (call, closed, open)

11 (away, gift, begin)   (present, there, play)

12 (shape, size, tall)   (long, high, small)

13 (temper, cross, peaceful)   (rough, calm, storm)

5

If the code for MATTER is 4 6 5 5 3 2, what are the codes for the following words?

14 MAT _____   15 TEA _____   16 ARM _____

17 RATE _____   18 TEAR _____

5

19–23 Rearrange the muddled words in capital letters so that each sentence makes sense.

Example There are sixty SNODCES SECONDS in a UTMINE MINUTE.

My TAC _____ loves SHIF _____ but my ODG _____ likes

TEAM _____. He SKBRA _____ when he is hungry.

5

Complete the following sentences by selecting the most sensible word from each group of words given in the brackets. Underline the words selected.

Example The (children, books, foxes) carried the (houses, books, steps) home from the (greengrocer, library, factory).

24 The boy (swam, slept, sat) and (burnt, cut, mended) his (knee, bike, dog).

25 There's a (blue, cold, purple) wind (walking, blowing, hooting) (inside, outside, between).

26 Have you (played, clicked, win) the (board, friend, game) on the (film, computer, kitchen)?

27 The (fish, swimmer, boat) (dived, surfed, fished) into the (net, pool, bath).

28 The (clock, cat, fridge) (cooked, hummed, ticked) on the (light, fire, shelf).

5

If these words were placed in alphabetical order, which word would come 4th?

Example anxiety   auction   ancient   axiomatic   auxiliary

29 cow   car   bee   boar   apple   _____

30 house   pudding   hamster   pie   quarter   _____

2

Paper 14

Tom is smaller than Kang and Kang is smaller than Leo.

1 Who is the smallest? _____

2 Who is the biggest? _____

Number the words in each line in alphabetical order.

3 bun ___   bed ___   bat ___   big ___   bog ___

4 sat ___   sit ___   such ___   set ___   slide ___

5 dig ___   dad ___   desk ___   dull ___   do ___

6 fig ___   feel ___   far ___   for ___   full ___

Underline the pair of words most similar in meaning.

Example   come, go   <u>roam, wander</u>   fear, fare

7 bottom, top   sand, stones   sad, sorry

8 play, work   neat, tidy   day, week

9 laugh, chuckle   good, bad   price, cheap

10 few, many   glad, happy   over, under

11 above, over   hard, soft   up, down

If the code for READS is 4 6 5 3 2, what are the codes for the following words?

12 ADD   _____

13 SAD   _____

14 SEA   _____

15 DEAR   _____

16 DARES _____

Underline the one word which **cannot be made** from the letters of the word in capital letters.

Example   S T A T I O N E R Y   stone   ration   <u>nation</u>   noisy

17 SWEATER   tease   wart   trace   sweet

18 RELATION   tale   told   ration   late

19 CUSTARD   star   crust   trade   stud

20 COMRADE   dear   comet   dram   raced

21 WEATHER   health   wet   thaw   tree

5

Find and underline the two words which need to change places for each sentence to make sense.

Example   She went to <u>letter</u> the <u>write</u>.

22 Make sure the pasta is boiling before you put the water in.

23 The police closed off the parade for the street.

24 Nick needed to use the computer to do homework his.

25 Catrin couldn't stop laughing when she saw that she was wearing shoes different two.

4

Change the first word of the third pair in the same way as the other pairs to give a new word.

Example   bind, hind   bare, hare   but, <u>hut</u>

26 ran, run   ban, bun   fan, _____

27 no, not   go, got   do, _____

28 pat, pet   bat, bet   sat, _____

29 cot, cut   pot, put   not, _____

30 rice, ice   pink, ink   face, _____

5

Paper 15

1–5 Write the following words in the correct groups.

yellow   leeks   brown   pink   peas

Vegetables   **Colours**

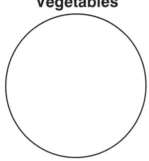

5

Rearrange the muddled words in capital letters to make sense.
They are all animals.

6 OGD   _____

7 BLMA   _____

8 PYON   _____

9 OATG   _____

10 ACT   _____

5

Remove one letter from the word in capital letters to leave a new word. The
meaning of the new word is given in the clue.

Example   A U N T   an insect   _ant_

11 CLOCK   you use a key in this   _____

12 PEACH   every one   _____

13 BOLD   opposite of young   _____

14 YEARS   we hear with these   _____

15 NESTS   fishermen use them   _____

5

Underline the word in the brackets which goes best with the words given outside the brackets.

Example   word, paragraph, sentence   (pen, cap, <u>letter</u>, top, stop)

16 page, cover, words   (television, book, poster, flower, photo)

17 board, dice, rules   (match, swim, laws, tired, game)

18 teacher, pupil, classroom   (bed, artist, school, shop, tree)

19 bus, truck, train   (car, chair, road, boxes, conductor)

20 robin, pigeon, magpie   (squirrel, seagull, mouse, snake, mole)   5

The first six letters of the alphabet are A B C D E F.

Take these letters out of the following words, then underline the words that would completely disappear.

Example   LOST   SHOE   <u>BEAD</u>   NEAT

21 DREAM   CRAFT   DEED   IDEAL

22 FLOOD   FACED   FIRE   FEET

23 DEAR   DREAD   AFTER   DEAF

24 FEED   CREED   CREAM   FATED   4

If a = 3, b = 4, c = 6, e = 9, find the value of:

25 c − b = _____

26 e − a = _____

27 a + b + c = _____   3

Find and underline the two words which need to change places for each sentence to make sense.

Example   She went to <u>letter</u> the <u>write</u>.

28 Lola ran to train the catch.

29 The tree blew the wind over.

30 He scored the final in the goal minute.   3

Now go to the Progress Chart to record your score!   Total   30

30

Find the four-letter word hidden at the end of one word and the beginning of the next word. The order of the letters may not be changed.

Example   The children had bats and balls.   *sand*

1 The game went into extra time.   _____

2 They left the sandy beach at five o'clock.   _____

3 We stayed at the hotel by the sea.   _____

4 We had to be at the station by six.   _____

5 One bear strayed out of the cave.   _____

5

Find the letter which willl end the first word and start the second word.

Example   peac (h) ome

6 the (__) any

7 fas (__) hin

8 cas (__) nee

9 hal (__) ish

10 bat (__) ard

5

Remove one letter from the word in capital letters to leave a new word. The meaning of the new word is given in the clue.

Example   A U N T   an insect   *ant*

11 STAND   it is on the beach   _____

12 BLINK   a piece in a chain   _____

13 BRAKE   to cook a cake   _____

14 SHOOT   to make a noise   _____

15 PANE   we use it when cooking   _____

5

Complete the following sentences by selecting the most sensible word from each group of words given in the brackets. Underline the words selected.

Example The (<u>children</u>, books, foxes) carried the (houses, <u>books</u>, steps) home from the (greengrocer, <u>library</u>, factory).

16 Dad (drank, read, cooked) the (cushion, magazine, chair) before he went to (bed, the river, storm).

17 Ruby (scared, enjoyed, wished) the (colourful, squib, sparkle) display of (swimming, fireworks, bonfire).

18 Why have you (left, planted, lost) your (friends, clothes, holidays) in the (sunshine, fridge, bathroom)?

19 The (boat, ships, cabin) was (washed, tossed, hurl) about on the stormy (wave, sea, beach).

20 The (cats, dogs, horses) (mooed, neighed, grunted) to be let out of their (kennel, stable, basket).

5

If a = 4, b = 6, c = 9, d = 12, find the value of:

21 $3a + b =$ _____

22 $c + d =$ _____

23 $d - a - b =$ _____

24 $c - b =$ _____

25 $a + a =$ _____

5

Underline two words, one from each group, that go together to form a new word. The word in the first group always comes first.

Example (hand, <u>green</u>, for) (light, <u>house</u>, sure)

26 (sky, sea, bird) (cloud, sand, gull)

27 (fair, light, ride) (star, ground, train)

28 (hose, sink, flag) (band, tap, pole)

29 (net, fish, cross) (work, rod, catch)

30 (draw, colour, paint) (box, hand, sew)

5

Change the first word of the third pair in the same way as the other pairs to give a new word.

Example bind, hind bare, hare but, <u>hut</u>

1 wan, wane ban, bane man, _____

2 man, men fan, fen pan, _____

3 bell, ball cell, call tell, _____

4 fill, fall hill, hall will, _____

5 pill, ill done, one sand, _____

5

Underline the word in the brackets closest in meaning to the word in capitals.

Example UNHAPPY (unkind laughter <u>sad</u> friendly)

6 TALE (read paper news story)

7 WALK (cycle skate stride run)

8 BREAK (tear bend dent shatter)

9 TRAVEL (foreign places journey plane)

10 NOISE (uproar crowd hush end)

5

Underline one word in the brackets which is most opposite in meaning to the word in capitals.

Example WIDE (broad long <u>narrow</u> motorway)

11 HARD (work soft sharp tough)

12 WILD (scary fierce tame find)

13 FOUND (try lost seek missed)

14 QUIET (bang silent hear loud)

4

Find the letter which will end the first word and start the second word.

Example   peac (<u>h</u>) ome

15 tre (—) ven

16 mes (—) ent

17 sto (—) ood

18 firs (—) op

19 spli (—) rip

○ 5

If a = 2, b = 3, c = 5, d = 10, give the answer to these calculations as letters.

20 a + b = _____

21 c − b = _____

22 d − c = _____

○ 3

If the code for STANCE is 1 3 5 7 9 8, what are the codes for the following words?

23 CATS   _____

24 ACES   _____

25 STATE   _____

What do these codes stand for?

26 1 8 3   _____

27 3 5 7   _____

○ 5

Megan and Yan like salad. Robin and Mark like pasta, Mark and Megan like apple pie. Yan and Robin like pizza

28 Who like pasta and pizza?   _____

29 Who likes salad and apple pie?   _____

30 Who likes pasta and apple pie?   _____

○ 3

Now go to the Progress Chart to record your score!   Total ○ 30

34

Which one letter can be added to the front of all of these words to make new words?

Example   c̲are   c̲at   c̲rate   c̲all

1 ___ot   ___ake   ___eal   ___abbit

2 ___late   ___ill   ___ie   ___uff

3 ___mell   ___ail   ___ky   ___kin

4 ___eat   ___at   ___igh   ___ouse

5 ___ig   ___rain   ___ive   ___en

⬭ 5

Find and underline the two words which need to change places for each sentence to make sense.

Example   She went to <u>letter</u> the <u>write</u>.

6 Ethan raced round the bike on his track.

7 The balloon floated the into sky.

8 The guide harness wore a yellow dog.

9 Her cold tingled with the fingers.

⬭ 4

Underline the two words which are the odd ones out in the following groups of words.

Example   black   <u>king</u>   purple   green   <u>house</u>

10 sob   wail   water   sea   cry

11 mug   stool   beaker   cup   chair

12 pen   paper   pencil   rubber   crayon

13 house   field   meadow   cottage   pasture

14 boat   ship   sea   canoe   ocean

⬭ 5

These words have been written in code, but the codes are not under the correct words.

TO	TOY	BOY	YOU	TOYS
325	1236	123	423	12

Write the codes under the correct words.

15 TO   **16** TOY   **17** BOY   **18** YOU   **19** TOYS

_____   _____   _____   _____   _____   ◯ 5

Find the letter which will end the first word and start the second word.

Example   peac (h) ome

20 ten (—) urn   **21** mea (—) oan

22 sen (—) ate   **23** pul (—) ady

24 pai (—) oar   **25** al (—) eat

26 bel (—) aw   **27** len (—) rum   ◯ 8

If e = 2, f = 4, g = 6, h = 8, give the answer to these calculations as letters.

28 e + f = _____

29 f + f = _____

30 h − g = _____   ◯ 3

Paper 19

Find the letter which will end the first word and start the second.

Example   peac (<u>h</u>) ome

1 car (___) ive

2 fal (___) awn

3 pla (___) ice

4 cuf (___) air

5 se (___) and

5

Complete the following sentences by selecting the most sensible word from each group of words given in the brackets. Underline the words selected.

Example   The (<u>children</u>, books, foxes) carried the (houses, <u>books</u>, steps) home from the (greengrocer, <u>library</u>, factory).

6 The (cup, chair, fork) is covered with (tall, floral, wide) (sacking, pattern, material).

7 We have three (dogs, pictures, cups) hanging on the (ceiling, lights, walls) of the (garage, shed, room).

8 Did you (always, ever, rare) swim in the (lake, pond, sea) with (boat, dolphins, ocean)?

9 The (pig, dragon, frog) had (babies, stones, scales) on its (back, teeth, cave).

10 Sean (squeezed, jumped, ran) under the (dog, road, gate) as (lazily, sadly, quickly) as he could.

5

Change one word so that the sentence makes sense. Underline the word you are taking out and write your new word on the line.

Example   I waited in line to buy a <u>book</u> to see the film.   *ticket*

11 Dad and I went to see the penguins and monkeys at the local jungle.   _____

12 Michael has broken the fingers and thumb of his left foot.   _____

13 The knife is very blunt so be careful you don't cut yourself.   _____

3

Find the four-letter word hidden at the end of one word and the beginning of the next word. The order of the letters may not be changed.

Example The children had bats and balls. _sand_

14 We are going to the park later. _____

15 Are there steps to climb? _____

16 The baby wasn't born early. _____

17 Ravi was playing with his brother. _____

18 When shall we leave for our holiday? _____

⬭ 5

Add one letter to the word in capital letters to make a new word. The meaning of the new word is given in the clue.

Example PLAN simple _plain_

19 LAP It is a kind of light. _____

20 RED We are taught to do this at school. _____

21 FOG A tadpole becomes this. _____

22 NET Birds live in it. _____

23 MAT It is part of a ship. _____

⬭ 5

Complete the following expressions by underlining the missing word.

Example Frog is to tadpole as swan is to (duckling, baby, <u>cygnet</u>).

24 Cheap is to expensive as open is to (money, shop, shut).

25 Cat is to kitten as sheep is to (wool, lamb, pup).

26 Hat is to head as glove is to (foot, leg, hand).

27 Big is to little as large is to (small, huge, enormous).

28 Go is to come as in is to (by, out, road).

⬭ 5

Number the words in each line in alphabetical order.

29 met ___ mat ___ mit ___ muck ___ mock ___

30 tug ___ tip ___ tell ___ tall ___ top ___

⬭ 2

Now go to the Progress Chart to record your score! Total ⬭ 30

38

Paper 20

Find a word that is similar in meaning to the word in capital letters and that rhymes with the second word.

Example   CABLE   tyre   *wire*

1 A DOG   sound   _____

2 A QUARREL   light   _____

3 TO BEGIN   chart   _____

4 A SMALL RODENT house   _____

5 A BOX   plate   _____

5

Find the letter that will end the first word and start the second word.

Example   peac (h) ome

6 ben (__) ea

7 boa (__) en

8 son (__) one

9 ram (__) ilot

10 see (__) rip

5

Remove one letter from the word in capital letters to leave a new word. The meaning of the new word is given in the clue.

Example   A U N T   an insect   *ant*

11 BEAT   you use it to hit a ball   _____

12 PLAIN   a throb, an ache   _____

13 SHARP   a musical instrument   _____

14 TRACE   you run in one of these   _____

15 BLEAR   an animal   _____

5

Underline one word in the brackets which is most opposite in meaning to the word in capitals.

Example   WIDE   (broad   long   <u>narrow</u>   motorway)

16 STRONG   (weak   hard   solid   light)

17 WELL   (water   happy   ill   fit)

18 HIGH   (wide   bottom   low   top)

19 COLD   (chill   hot   warm   boil)

20 FIRST   (last   front   back   lose)

5

Answer these questions. The alphabet has been given to help you.

A B C D E F G H I J K L M N O P Q R S T U V W X Y Z

21 Which letter is as many places after L as H is after C?   ___

22 Make a word from the 12th, 5th, 1st and 4th letters.   _____

23 Make a word from the 4th, 1st, 13th and 5th letters.   _____

24 Which letter is as many places from the beginning as W is from the end?   ___

4

25 Today is Wednesday 30th December.

On which day will the New Year start?   _____

26 Yesterday was Monday 23rd December.

Christmas Day will be on which day?   _____

2

Find a word that can be put in front of each of the following words to make new, compound words.

Example   CAST   FALL   WARD   POUR   <u>DOWN</u>

27 BIRD   FOOD   FRONT   BED   _____

28 BOAT   TIME   BELT   LIKE   _____

29 BERRY   OUT   BIRD   MAIL   _____

30 DRESS   SHIP   AXE   FIELD   _____

4

Paper 21

Fill in the crosswords so that all the given words are included. You have been given one letter as a clue in each crossword.

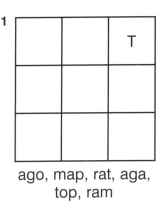

ago, map, rat, aga, top, ram

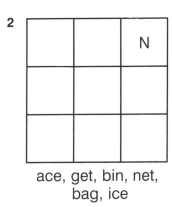

ace, get, bin, net, bag, ice

○2

Add one letter to the word in capital letters to make a new word. The meaning of the new word is given in the clue.

Example   PLAN   simple   *plain*

3 BIND   unable to see   _____

4 COST   on the beach   _____

5 SOW   not as fast   _____

6 BAD   having no hair   _____

7 EARN   understand how to do things   _____

○5

If the code for STORED is A C D F H I, what are the codes for the following words?

8 DOT _____   9 RED _____   10 ORE _____

11 REST _____   12 DOTES _____

○5

13–17 Look at these groups of words.

A   B   C   D
Vegetables   Buildings   Things we do   Birds

Choose the correct group for each of the words below. Write in the letter.

house ___   owl ___   cycle ___   run ___   write ___

lark ___   onions ___   swan ___   school ___   leeks ___

○5

41

Rearrange the muddled words in capital letters so that each sentence makes sense.

Example There are sixty SNODCES <u>SECONDS</u> in a UTMINE <u>MINUTE</u>.

18–20 NHEW _____ are you GNLFYI _____ to DANII _____?

21–22 Be CIUKQ _____ or you will be late for the AMINCE _____. ◯ 5

Complete the following sentences by selecting the most sensible word from each group of words given in the brackets. Underline the words selected.

Example The (<u>children</u>, books, foxes) carried the (houses, <u>books</u>, steps) home from the (greengrocer, <u>library</u>, factory).

23 Ali gets out his (cot, bag, box) to return his (sweets, DVDs, drinks) to the (library, theatre, surgery).

24 Don't (drop, throw, touch) the (wall, book, fence). It is (lost, small, electric).

25 The (grass, cloud, sea) was (rushing, waving, crashing) on the (floor, road, shore).

26 He (gobbled, pushed, stole) the (tower, pudding, door) (badly, sadly, greedily).

27 The (teacher, postman, violinist) brought Anna a (parcel, music, drink) for her birthday. ◯ 5

28 If April 1st was a Friday, what day was the 31st March? _____

29 My watch is 5 minutes fast. If my watch shows it is 12.30, what is the real time? _____

30 My birthday is on the 12th. John's birthday is four days after Ranvir's. Ranvir's birthday is the day before mine. What is the date of John's birthday? _____ ◯ 3

Now go to the Progress Chart to record your score! Total ◯ 30

Find the letter that will end the first word and start the second word.

    Example   peac (<u>h</u>) ome

1 cor (___) rain

2 pe (___) ib

3 foo (___) hen

4 sea (___) ion

5 tow (___) ote

    5

Underline two words, one from each group, that go together to form a new word. The word in the first group always comes first.

    Example   (hand, <u>green</u>, for)   (light, <u>house</u>, sure)

6 (skin, jaw, front)   (spring, back, bone)

7 (bag, field, song)   (lark, pipes, hill)

8 (fort, flow, draw)   (bridge, road, water)

    3

Add one letter to the word in capital letters to make a new word. The meaning of the new word is given in the clue.

    Example   PLAN   simple   *plain*

9 FAST   a lot of food   _____

10 FAIL   not very strong   _____

11 PANT   something that grows in the garden   _____

12 LATE   something we use at meal times   _____

13 SIP   to fall   _____

14 PEAK   to talk   _____

15 RIGHT   to have a scare   _____

    7

Find a word that is similar in meaning to the word in capital letters and that rhymes with the second word.

    Example   CABLE   tyre   *wire*

16 INSTRUCT   peach   _____

17 GRAZE   hatch   _____

18 BROOK   dream   _____

19 RAIL CARRIAGES   stain   _____

20 SEASHORE   toast   _____   **5**

Complete the following expressions by underlining the missing word.

    Example   Frog is to tadpole as swan is to (duckling, baby, <u>cygnet</u>).

21 Hoof is to horse as claw is to (zebra, cat, goat).

22 Flower is to garden as fish is to (stall, net, sea).

23 Cook is to stove as drive is to (bike, lane, car).

24 Croak is to frog as cluck is to (hen, owl, raven).

25 Plane is to sky as boat is to (float, sail, water).   **5**

If the code for ORANGE is LPXBQF, what are the codes for the following words?

26 NAG   _____

27 RAG   _____

28 ORE   _____

What do these codes stand for?

29 QFXP   _____

30 PXBQ   _____   **5**

Progress Chart   Verbal Reasoning 7-8 years

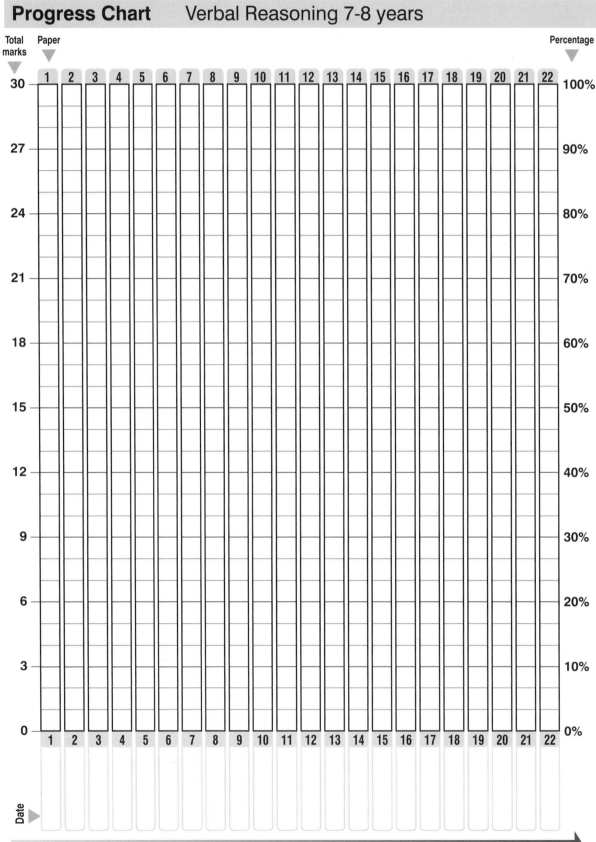

When you've finished the book read the Next Steps